TO: MY AMANDA

LOVE DEBS

FROM: XOXO

Friends

WRITTEN AND COMPILED BY

Barbara Paulding AND
Rene J. Smith

 PETER PAUPER PRESS, INC.
White Plains, New York

Designed by La Shae V. Ortiz

Copyright © 2011
Peter Pauper Press, Inc.
202 Mamaroneck Avenue
White Plains, NY 10601
All rights reserved
ISBN 978-1-4413-0530-5
Printed in China
7 6 5 4 3 2 1

Visit us at www.peterpauper.com

Friends

Introduction

Friendship is born at that moment when one person says to another, "What! You too? I thought I was the only one."

—C.S. LEWIS

Here's to the friends who believe in us, those "second selves" who see us through, the good companions we

can count on, come what may.
Filled with uplifting quotations
that explore and honor friendship,
this wise and witty little book is
the perfect tribute to true friends
everywhere.

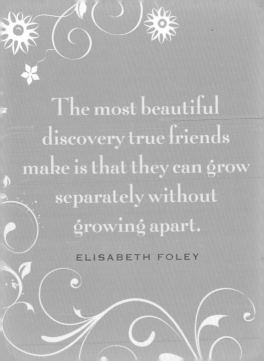

The most beautiful
discovery true friends
make is that they can grow
separately without
growing apart.

ELISABETH FOLEY

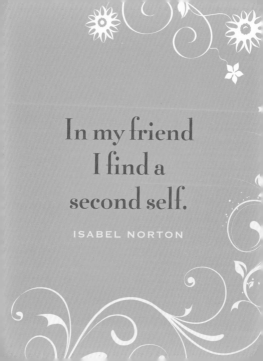

In my friend
I find a
second self.

ISABEL NORTON

A joy that's shared is a joy made double.

ENGLISH PROVERB

There is one friend in
the life of each of us who
seems not a separate person,
however dear and beloved,
but an expansion,
an interpretation, of one's self,
the very meaning of
one's soul.

EDITH WHARTON

I believe that everyone is the keeper of a dream—and by tuning into one another's secret hopes, we can become better friends, better partners, better parents, and better lovers.

OPRAH WINFREY

A friend is a gift you give yourself.

ROBERT LOUIS STEVENSON

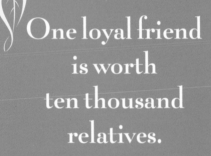

One loyal friend
is worth
ten thousand
relatives.

EURIPEDES

A true friend
is one soul in
two bodies.

ARISTOTLE

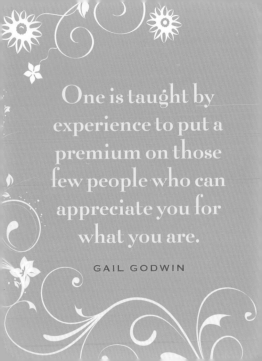

One is taught by
experience to put a
premium on those
few people who can
appreciate you for
what you are.

GAIL GODWIN

You can always tell
a real friend; when you've
made a fool of yourself he
doesn't feel you've done a
permanent job.

LAURENCE J. PETER

A good friend is a
connection to life—a tie to
the past, a road to the future,
the key to sanity in a totally
insane world.

LOIS WYSE

One's friends are
that part of the
human race with which
one can be human.

GEORGE SANTAYANA

Friendship is born from an identity of spiritual goals—from common navigation toward a star.

ANTOINE
DE SAINT-EXUPÉRY

Nine-tenths of
the people were created
so you would want to be
with the other tenth.

HORACE WALPOLE

Friendship is a heart-flooding feeling that can happen to any two people who are caught up in the act of being themselves, together.

LETTY COTTIN POGREBIN

Some people go
to priests; others
to poetry;
I to my friends.

VIRGINIA WOOLF

We cherish our friends
not for their ability to
amuse us, but for ours
to amuse them.

EVELYN WAUGH

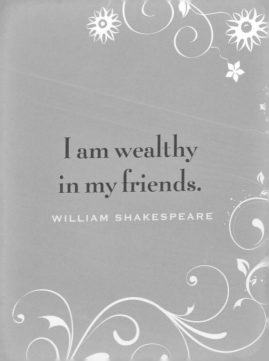

I am wealthy
in my friends.

WILLIAM SHAKESPEARE

A true friend is the most precious of all possessions and the one we take the least thought about acquiring.

LA ROCHEFOUCAULD

Be slow to fall into
friendship; but when
thou art in, continue
firm and constant.

SOCRATES

We should behave to our
friends as we would wish our
friends to behave to us.

ARISTOTLE

Sometimes being a friend means
mastering the art of timing.
There is a time for silence.
A time to let go and allow
people to hurl themselves into
their own destiny.
And a time to prepare to pick up
the pieces when it's all over.

GLORIA NAYLOR

We're not primarily on this earth to see through one another, but to see one another through.

PETER DE VRIES

In life you throw a ball.
You hope it will reach a
wall and bounce back so
you can throw it again.
You hope your friends
will provide that wall.

PABLO PICASSO

Friendship is love minus sex and plus reason. Love is friendship plus sex and minus reason.

MASON COOLEY

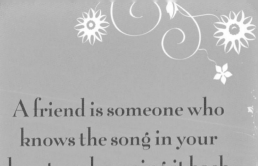

A friend is someone who knows the song in your heart, and can sing it back to you when you have forgotten the words.

DONNA ROBERTS

Friends are relatives you make for yourself.

EUSTACHE DESCHAMPS

When you're in jail,
a good friend will be
trying to bail you out.
A best friend will be in
the cell next to you saying,
"Damn, that was fun."

GROUCHO MARX

The trouble is
not in dying for a
friend, but in
finding a friend
worth dying for.

MARK TWAIN

The best way to
destroy an
enemy is to make
him a friend.

ABRAHAM LINCOLN

In everyone's life,
at some time, our inner
fire goes out. It is then
burst into flame by an
encounter with another
human being. We should
all be thankful for those
people who rekindle
the inner spirit.

ALBERT SCHWEITZER

Friendship is born at
that moment when one
person says to another,
"What! You too? I thought
I was the only one."

C. S. LEWIS

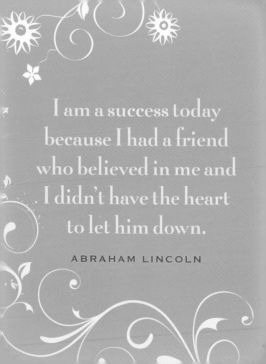

I am a success today
because I had a friend
who believed in me and
I didn't have the heart
to let him down.

ABRAHAM LINCOLN

Iron sharpeneth iron;
so a man sharpeneth
the countenance of
his friend.

PROVERBS 27:17

The friend who holds
your hand and says the
wrong thing is made of
dearer stuff than the
one who stays away.

BARBARA KINGSOLVER

To me, fair friend, you can never be old.

WILLIAM SHAKESPEARE

The holy passion of friendship is so sweet and steady and loyal and enduring in nature that it will last through a whole lifetime, if not asked to lend money.

MARK TWAIN

Friends outlast trends.

SUZANNE SIEGEL ZENKEL

And do as adversaries
do in law—
strive mightily,
but eat and drink
as friends.

WILLIAM SHAKESPEARE,
The Taming of the Shrew

From wine what
sudden friendship
springs!

JOHN GAY

My true friends have
always given me that
supreme proof of devotion,
a spontaneous aversion for
the man I loved.

COLETTE

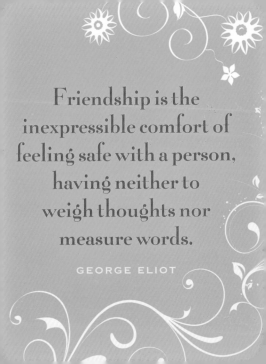

Friendship is the inexpressible comfort of feeling safe with a person, having neither to weigh thoughts nor measure words.

GEORGE ELIOT

We are friends and I do like to pass the day with you in serious and inconsequential chatter. I wouldn't mind washing up beside you, dusting beside you, reading the back half of the paper while you read the front.

JEANETTE WINTERSON

Love is blind.
Friendship tries
not to notice.

AUTHOR UNKNOWN

Platonic friendship:
The interval between
the introduction and
the first kiss.

SOPHIE IRENE LOEB

She had yet to learn how often intimacies between women go backwards, beginning with revelations and ending up in small talk without loss of esteem.

ELIZABETH BOWEN

A friend that ain't
in need is a
friend indeed.

KIN HUBBARD

There is nothing better than a friend, unless it is a friend with chocolate.

CHARLES DICKENS

We are all travelers
in the wilderness
of this world, and the best
we can find in our travels
is an honest friend.

ROBERT LEWIS STEVENSON

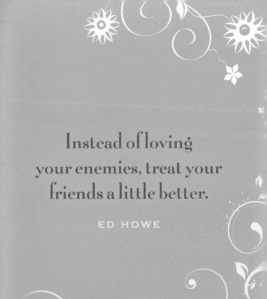

Instead of loving
your enemies, treat your
friends a little better.

ED HOWE

Love thy neighbor as thyself, but choose your neighborhood.

LOUISE BEAL

The imaginary friends
I had as a kid dropped me
because their friends
thought I didn't exist.

AARON MACHADO

'Tis the privilege of
friendship to talk nonsense,
and have her nonsense
respected.

CHARLES LAMB

Anyway, just because
you're sworn enemies
doesn't mean you can't be
friends, does it?

TERRY PRATCHETT

One good reason to only maintain a small circle of friends is that three out of four murders are committed by people who know the victim.

GEORGE CARLIN

The best mirror is
an old friend.

GEORGE HERBERT

I love everything that's old:
old friends, old times,
old manners, old books,
old wine.

OLIVER GOLDSMITH,
She Stoops to Conquer

Friends love you,
warts and all.

AUTHOR UNKNOWN

Words were never
invented to fully explain
the peaceful aura that
surrounds us when we are
in communion with minds
of the same thoughts.

EDDIE MYERS

Friendship is
Love without
his wings.

LORD BYRON

Friends drop
in when others
drop out.

SUZANNE SIEGEL ZENKEL

The proper office of a friend
is to side with you when
you are wrong. Nearly
anybody will side with you
when you are right.

MARK TWAIN

Remember, the greatest gift is not found in a store nor under a tree, but in the hearts of true friends.

CINDY LEW

A friend can
tell you things you
don't want to
tell yourself.

FRANCES WARD WELLER

I would rather walk
with a friend in the
dark than walk alone
in the light.

HELEN KELLER

There are people in my life who give me comfort when the going gets tough, as it invariably does.... They will lift me up when I fall, they will hold me in their arms as I cry and tell me everything's going to be okay. I am so thankful for those people; they are priceless.

AUTHOR UNKNOWN

It is easier to forgive
an enemy than to
forgive a friend.

WILLIAM BLAKE

Friends ... cherish one
another's hopes.
They are kind to one
another's dreams.

HENRY DAVID THOREAU

Friendship is always
a sweet responsibility,
never an opportunity.

KAHLIL GIBRAN

Friendship is a
sheltering tree.

SAMUEL TAYLOR COLERIDGE

A friend is one
who knows us, but
loves us anyway.

FATHER JEROME CUMMINGS

Laugh and the world
laughs with you.
Cry and you cry with
your girlfriends.

LAURIE KUSLANSKY

I've learned that people will forget what you said, people will forget what you did, but people will never forget how you made them feel.

MAYA ANGELOU

Each friend represents
a world in us, a world
possibly not born until
they arrive, and it is only
by this meeting that a
new world is born.

ANAÏS NIN

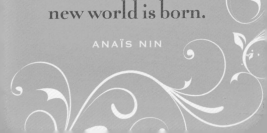

A single rose
can be my garden . . .
a single friend,
my world.

LEO BUSCAGLIA

Old friends cannot be created out of hand. Nothing can match the treasure of common memories, of trials endured together, of quarrels and reconciliations and generous emotions. It is idle, having planted an acorn in the morning, to expect that afternoon to sit in the shade of the oak.

ANTOINE
DE SAINT-EXUPÉRY

I have learned that
to be with those
I like is enough.

WALT WHITMAN

Friendship is the
only cement that will
ever hold the world
together.

WOODROW WILSON

Greater love has
no man than this,
that a man
lay down his life
for his friends.

JOHN 15:13

Everyone hears what you say.
Friends listen to what you
say. Best friends listen to
what you don't say.

AUTHOR UNKNOWN

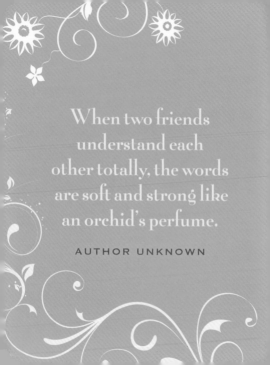

When two friends
understand each
other totally, the words
are soft and strong like
an orchid's perfume.

AUTHOR UNKNOWN

My best friend
is the one that
brings out the
best in me.

HENRY FORD

Winning has always
meant much to me,
but winning friends
has meant the most.

Hold a true friend
with both your hands.

NIGERIAN PROVERB

It is not often that someone comes along who is a true friend and a good writer.

E. B. WHITE,
Charlotte's Web

When all is said and done,
it is the people in your life,
the friendships you form
and the commitments
you maintain, that give
shape to your life.

HILLARY RODHAM CLINTON

We will surely
get to our destination
if we join hands.

AUNG SAN SUU KYI

Even though we've changed and we're all finding our own place in the world, we all know that . . . no matter where this crazy world takes us, nothing will ever change so much to the point where we're not all still friends.

ALLISON MOSHER

Gentle ladies, you will
remember till old age what
we did together in our
brilliant youth!

SAPPHO

Take care of friendships,
hold people you love close
to you, take advantage
of birthdays to
celebrate fiercely.

PATTI LABELLE

"We'll be Friends
Forever, won't we, Pooh?"
asked Piglet.
"Even longer,"
Pooh answered.

A. A. MILNE